Lifting of the Veil

Meghan Warner

BookLeaf
Publishing

India | USA | UK

Lifting of the Veil © 2024 Meghan Warner

All rights reserved.

No part of this publication may be reproduced, stored in a retrieval system, or transmitted, in any form or by any means, electronic, mechanical, photocopying, recording or otherwise, without the prior written permission of the presenters.

Meghan Warner asserts the moral right to be identified as author of this work.

Presentation by *BookLeaf Publishing*

Web: www.bookleafpub.com

E-mail: info@bookleafpub.com

ISBN: 9789360942731

First edition 2024

To the man, lover, father, best friend and husband who believes in me more than I could ever believe in myself. Thank you for showing me the way love should feel.

To my sweet sons, Van, Henry and Sawyer, may you always face the headwinds straight on and know yourselves to be true. You are my North Star, dear ones.

Kennebunkport

You wanted to see the Ocean
frozen and fierce on the Maine coast
sitting shelves of summer granite
now battering stones for icy waves

We stood on the beach shivering
wild wind whispering speckles
of saltwater in-between the folds
of our coats.

Raw and bitter the January gray
enveloping us like a snow globe
inescapable and heavy. The Ocean
dark, roiling threatening, calling

Out to me, reminding me I
cannot outrun the darkness
beneath.

You snored, your clothes still on
as I drank the bottle meant for us
Silent tears that could melt
the frozen Atlantic

I was moored, unable to sink
or swim.

Clouds

A Carly Simon record scratched
"Clouds in my coffee and you're so vain"
You sang off tune, making up lyrics
humming the parts you didn't know

Sloppy drunk, loose hips swaying
the arthritis in your knuckles
bending your fingers like branches

A lighter, freer version of my father
Not quite as heavy with melancholy
happy in the void of too many Miller lites,
reminiscing about reckless youthful adventure

When did he become human?
Closing the bedroom door, unsure how to help
his teenage daughter, his black mustache
catching tears on a cloudy Monday morning

Was that the crack between parent & child?
A widening chasm that love alone couldn't
traverse
when he became another casualty
to my steam train of independence

I want to hold him now, tell him he did his best
tell him how much I love him, how I forgive him

I lean back instead, admiring the freedom
he feels and promising to tell him
someday
soon

Summer 2005

Steam from the shrimp bisque
mists the sweat from chef's forehead
as he machine-gun fires dinner specials:
coq au vin, duck (medium rare, no exceptions)
Our bodies nearly touching, hunched over
whispering about the couple at Table 5,
counting $20s into stacks
at the end our shift. Greedy for more.

We drank whiskey & ginger ale, shooting
pool, stacking quarters on the filthy edge
between drags of Marlboro lights and
thought to ourselves: this must be freedom.

Your fingers dancing along the curve of my hips,
hips I didn't even know I had until your touch.
I sank desperately deep to the bottom, anchoring
into delusions of desire. Falling asleep while the
world was waking up,
birds blessing the rising sun
and our entwined bodies

That first love, memories catching in your throat
decades later, of skipped
heartbeats, sweaty palms, skin tingling

from the inside, without the knowledge

of how it ends.

Daffodil Yellow

the glorious way Spring is more a feeling than a
season

barefoot, the Earth holds you
a deep inhale, dank dirty
delightful

an orchestra of spring peepers
heralds in a new beginning,
a sigh of relief

can you feel it? the buzzy
almost manic enchantment
of the sun

there's magic all around,
as if everyone has a secret
they're desperate to tell

Spring delivers slippery promises
on the wings of Robins, as hope
of a bright year lands in all

our hearts

Emergence

Tectonic plates of my pelvis
shifting, separating
expanding

how can this be right?

Your tiny body
exquisitely huge

And the veil lifts,
moments before
your delicate, rose petal
body slipped
into this world,
into my hands.

A heartbeat glimmer
of when we were still one
body

And then, there you were: dark bright eyes
of amazing clarity, knowing exactly
why you are here
why you are mine

Blood drying between my legs
breasts swollen, breathing in
slow motion

I felt my soul come back
(even though I hadn't known it was missing)
Emerging anew, reborn

God

Salvation on a Sunday morning,
in worn out oak pews
kneeling in unison.

Performance art.

Secretly judging, casting eyes,
whispering gossip
between hymnals.

The cruel pinch from my mother's
fingers as my attention drifted
to more pressing questions:

Why does God have to be a man?
(and why does that feel wrong?)
Why do I have to seek God here?

Isn't God in the cool steam, shocking
royal sunsets of late August
In the coils of my fingerprints
and the juicy rolls of a baby's thighs

Isn't God anywhere but here?

Where we wear masks to hide
our judging and meddling
Explaining our sins,
promising to be better
tomorrow. Already a lie.

My "God" is not here.
My God is waiting for me
with compassion, patience
understanding for all I have
lost to man's "church"

My God is doesn't offer love
in the form of punishment

Inner Child

I grew those hands, but they are not mine
They belong to the stars and moon.
His eyes liquid pools of ancestors old.

Who am I to think he owed me
any greater gift than who he is here to be.
Who am I to force my will on his pure soul?

I glimpsed her today. In rage, frustration
with my son's weepy pleas, illogic meltdowns,
I heard my mother's words, felt her wounds

In his pain, confusion, overwhelm, I saw her.
Reaching out for me, asking for compassion
a tender embrace, a gentle wiping of her tears

My chest broke open, throat tightened
was I drowning or rising, from that dark place?
She called from the past, coiled in the cries

Of my son, twisting through my buzzing anger
My quick, burning words, rough rote hugs
Impatient, growling sighs transformed

When I saw my young self in the tears

of my son's almond brown eyes.
Holding the small, heavy weight of my child

I held generations of children
who received a hard hand, instead of a hug.
I held a little girl who needed me to love her.

King-sized

Discarded, wrapped in plastic
Crinkling in the wind.
I made you turn around
Haul it into the truck bed, pleased
with my keen eyes & your bold brawn.

Our bed. King-sized love
Free and meant to be. Do you remember?
Long, luxurious evenings intertwined
No worries of what's for dinner or endless
household chores,
curious and connected we escaped
in our island bed

Now there is we. Between us
miniature toes, toothless grins
hourless nights that became weeks, years.
You're a shadow in early morning hours,
slipping away to the day.

I long to call out, remind you our sheets
won't always smell of breastmilk & baby heads.
Encase you in the memory of when
I only had you to love.

When king-sized was big enough.

Choose Your Plot Wisely

There is no way to describe
the aliveness of dirt
between my fingers, breaking clumps
of soil, moist, dense yet
flowing effortlessly down to the ground
a safe, gentle womb for teardrop
green bean seeds, minuscule carrot
seeds lost, until delicate green
strands of life emerge,
signaling growth from below.

Isn't it amazing what happens where we cannot
see?

Sweet tendril roots seeking support,
an entire life happening beneath.

How many of us walk around
hiding our growth,
petrified to stand out,
avoiding the bright light of scrutiny?

What we gardeners know is
with time, nourishment and care
even the weakest seedling can
grow the biggest bloom.

Modern Motherhood

They lied.
When they said we could have it all.

If we didn't ask too many questions,
challenge authority, as long as we
accommodated, massaged the egos
kept our needs quiet & small

As long as we were good little girls

There is an angry woman inside of me
Generations of angry women, lurching
clawing for a voice that matters
I feel them at the edge of a sentence
I did not finish to save someone's feelings
or an apology that bookends all my needs

"I'm sorry my needs are inconvenient. I'm sorry
my guilt gets in the way of helping myself get
what I need. I was taught to put everyone else
before myself."

They told us we should make money. While also
growing, birthing, raising babies.

While cooking, cleaning, folding, offering
smiles at the PTA & joy at playground meetups.
While drowning in tantrums, emails, emotional
& intellectual needs of others piling up all
around you. While you bob dangerously below
the surface, praying someone will toss you a life
vest.

Because we all know, mothers cannot ask for
one.

What they didn't tell us, was that ALL, simply
meant more.

With a smile.

Yes, We Cosleep

I wasn't supposed to

This wasn't supposed to happen

I was putting you at risk,
that's what they told me

The way I carried this secret
shame, imagining the worst
believing their fear

But you gave me no choice

Screaming for me at all hours,
refusing to settle until you heard
my heartbeat
Even then,
it wasn't always enough

There came a bright winter day,
both crying, you behind the prison
(I mean crib)
Me, holding your tender, tiny hand
Through the slats
Those brown eyes full of confusion

"Mommy, why won't you pick me up?"

My sweet baby who I finally, mercifully
can call my own,
yet I deny him my comfort?
For who? For a society who tells me to
abandon my baby every day for 8 hours,
When we are still so new to each other,
In love, enchanted, bonded
Be careful, they say
Don't want a child too dependent on you
For comfort & sleep

And safety

When we abandon them at night,
We are telling them, they are not
As important as the sleep we need
To work

My sweet child, you are not more important than
the money
I need to pay for you

I revolt
I bring you into our bed
Your sweaty mass of black hair
Nestled in my arm pit

My body wrapped around yours
Protecting & calming you
Your entire body releases, relaxes
Knows you are so loved

That day I decided to never leave you
And what I was "supposed to do"
Could go fuck itself

On the Corner of Ashland and Bryant, 2016

You asked to kiss me
Which I thought was weird
And sorta cute
I leaned into your
barrel chest and found myself
quite surprised at the gentleness
of your hand at the small of my back,
the softness of your lips
the beam of your smile afterwards
and how I felt nothing

I didn't feel compelled to obsess
over every text I wrote, rewriting a million
times or replaying conversations
I didn't second guess myself
or tunnel into the dark hole
of anxiety and self-shame
I was entirely comfortable,
calm, unexcited

This wasn't how love felt,
was it?
At least no love I had
ever known

I knew I had fallen
when I recognized my
uncertainly was actually
safety

It wasn't until he asked me for a kiss,
on a Friday night in the cool of spring
under the streetlight

That I finally knew I what it felt
to be safe

A Wish

I wish I could remember

the smell of your head
feel the weight of your tiny body
entirely dependent on…me

your precious fingers unfurling
like palms of a fern in Spring
squeaks and squawks, a language
only we shared in the early days

I wish I could remember

your first real steps, alone
out in the world, away from me
Or when your babbles transformed
into words and wants

when the curls at the nape
of your neck, straightened
And your thigh rolls thinned

I wish I could remember

when your puffy baby

cheeks yielded to defined
features of a child

The thuds of fast feet
running through the halls
chased by pirates or dinosaurs

I wish I could remember

Every single moment
with absolute clarity
But it's a muddled mess
of adult to-dos & overwhelm

I wish I could remember

What my heart feels

Marlboro Lights

A rectangular ritual
smack the base of my hand
to get the perfect pack
I learned it from Dennis
at the bar, of course

Pull the aluminum foil
To reveal the white butts,
all in a perfect line
reminiscent
of a box of crayons

That first cigarette
from a fresh pack
there was almost a sense
of wonder swirling
in the smoke

Maybe it was the
deception of youth
Or the promise of escape

That romanticized a killer

Either way, there are days
I miss them
And who I thought I was

Emotional Manipulation

Get on your back and push
We have to check your cervix
We won't allow you to eat
We need to break your waters
Nothing good happens past 40 weeks
Baby is too big; you'll need a C-section

You can't say no to our policy
If you do, your baby will die
We know what's best
We're the professionals
Trust us

Where are the generations of women
screaming inside as their intuition
quietly rages against the system
that seeks to oppress and dismiss
their inner knowing and power

Women labelled
 "difficult" "too much"
"unrealistic" "irresponsible"
for questioning what doesn't
feel right, for wanting to know
why they should lie down, open

their legs when they're told to
like good little girls

Where are the women who want the
world to know

Birth belongs to them

Generational Trauma

Dear Mom,

Forgiveness comes to mind.
For your anxiety and fear
disguised as rage, for the times
your hands hurt rather than helped,
when your words broke off pieces
of my worth

I forgive your father and his fists
I forgive his mother and her hateful heart

I release these parts of me. I will not bury
them in dirty silence. I dredge these hurts
into the light to see the brokenness
was not my fault

Nor yours

Your grandchildren show you the way
I see how tenderly you care for them
and some day I will be brave enough
to ask,

      Do you wish you could have loved me
better?

I hope you will say yes.

A Haiku to my Husband

Your body and mine
wrapped together as one
to create three sons

The Lighthouse Road

The first time I ate mushrooms,
golden pink clouds billowed
and bloomed beyond the
horizon of Lake Ontario

Giggles hung in the air
between us, I felt as though
I was being swept away
to an unimaginable peace

Rocks digging into our backs
As we paddled our toes in
the cold October water,
our hands clasped together

Above us loomed the 150 year old
Lighthouse, its light still signaling
passing time as a battering ram
for wind water and ice

I wonder how many lives that
unfailing light has saved as we
make our way back up the
Lighthouse road, towards home

Back to small town suffocation,
hiding ourselves in the flock
desperate for a light to save us

www.ingramcontent.com/pod-product-compliance
Lightning Source LLC
La Vergne TN
LVHW010843200726
843508LV00012B/2728